The Severson Sisters Super Girl Guide To

PEER PRESSURE™

The Severson Sisters
Super Girl Guide To

PEER PRESSURE™

Your Action Plan to Create
Your Own Safe and Fabulous
Place in the World

The Severson Sisters

NEW YORK

The Severson Sisters Super Girl Guide To

PEER PRESSURE™

Connect to the Super Girl Within You

Published in New York, New York, by Morgan James Publishing. Morgan James and The Entrepreneurial Publisher are trademarks of Morgan James, LLC. www.MorganJamesPublishing.com

The Morgan James Speakers Group can bring authors to your live event. For more information or to book an event visit The Morgan James Speakers Group at www.TheMorganJamesSpeakersGroup.com.

A **free** eBook edition is available with the purchase of this print book.

CLEARLY PRINT YOUR NAME ABOVE IN UPPER CASE

Instructions to claim your free eBook edition:
1. Download the BitLit app for Android or iOS
2. Write your name in **UPPER CASE** on the line
3. Use the BitLit app to submit a photo
4. Download your eBook to any device

ISBN 978-1-63047-692-2 paperback
ISBN 978-1-63047-692-2 eBook
Library of Congress Control Number:
2015910989

Cover Design by:
Rachel Lopez
www.r2cdesign.com

Interior Design by:
Bonnie Bushman
The Whole Caboodle Graphic Design

In an effort to support local communities and raise awareness and funds, Morgan James Publishing donates a percentage of all book sales for the life of each book to Habitat for Humanity Peninsula and Greater Williamsburg.

Get involved today, visit
www.MorganJamesBuilds.com

Habitat
for Humanity®
Peninsula and
Greater Williamsburg
Building Partner

Peer pressure can be hard to deal with. It can bring up many emotions, both positive and negative. Peer pressure is part of growing up, and our goal with this book is to help you understand it better and provide you some options of how to handle peer pressure in your life. Remember, you ARE a Super Girl!

All our best,
The Severson Sisters Team

Table of Contents

Foreword

The *Severson Sisters Super Girl Workbook* is a lighthearted and creative solution to help you know how to handle peer pressure.

This workbook was developed by Severson Sisters and its Advisory Board. Severson Sisters is headquartered in Phoenix, Arizona and is an empowerment organization for girls. Our mission is to inspire girls to live as their awesome, authentic super selves!

Our Advisory Board is made up of educators, counselors, and a child psychologist.

Thank you to everyone who put their time and energy into this workbook. Thank you to every individual who donated to Severson Sisters to help this curriculum become the foundation for this workbook.

And thank you to every corporate partner who supported Severson Sisters; we are grateful to you.

We are able to do what we do because of all of you.

Thank you so very much!
The Severson Sisters Team

Preface

We define a Super Girl as a girl who is respectable, compassionate, and authentic in all ways. Super Girls are about peers—NOT peer pressure!

Be a Super Girl!

CHAPTER
1

Ground Rules

We're so excited for you to begin! Follow this curriculum step-by-step to get the most out of the Severson Sisters program.

We have a few ground rules that we set with our girls before each program begins. We encourage you to follow these rules as well.

The ground rules are:

1. It's best to be open and honest. There is no judgment at any point in this workbook.
2. This program is lighthearted. Remember to turn on some fun music and keep the positive energy going strong.
3. Enjoy every single second!
4. Get creative whenever possible.
5. Everyone MUST say their Super Girl Promise aloud and promise to follow through with it.

CHAPTER 2

The Timing of Super Girls

This workbook is written with the best of intentions. This is meant to be a fun and positive learning experience for YOU about YOU.

We recommend that you do the Super Girl Workbook at your own pace!

Severson Sisters!

CHAPTER 3

Confidence Star Policy and Super Girl Promise Cards

We ask you to remember our five key points as you enjoy this workbook: Safety, Honesty, Creativity, Openness, and Fun.

Please sign your name in the middle of your Confidence Star and keep it near you as you complete this workbook.

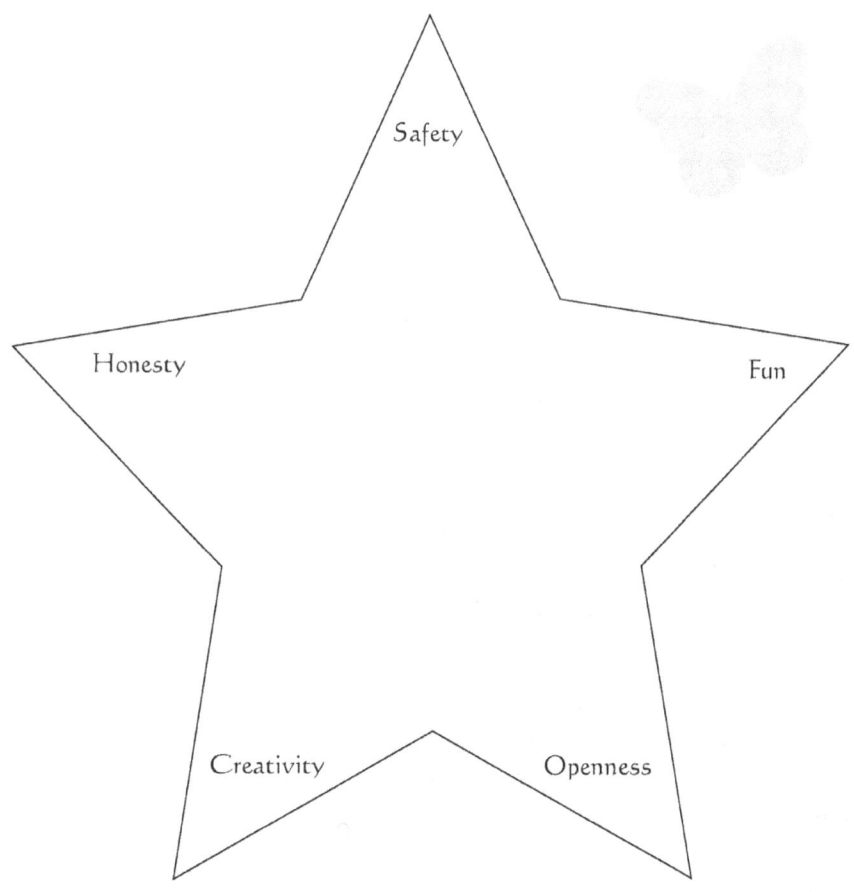

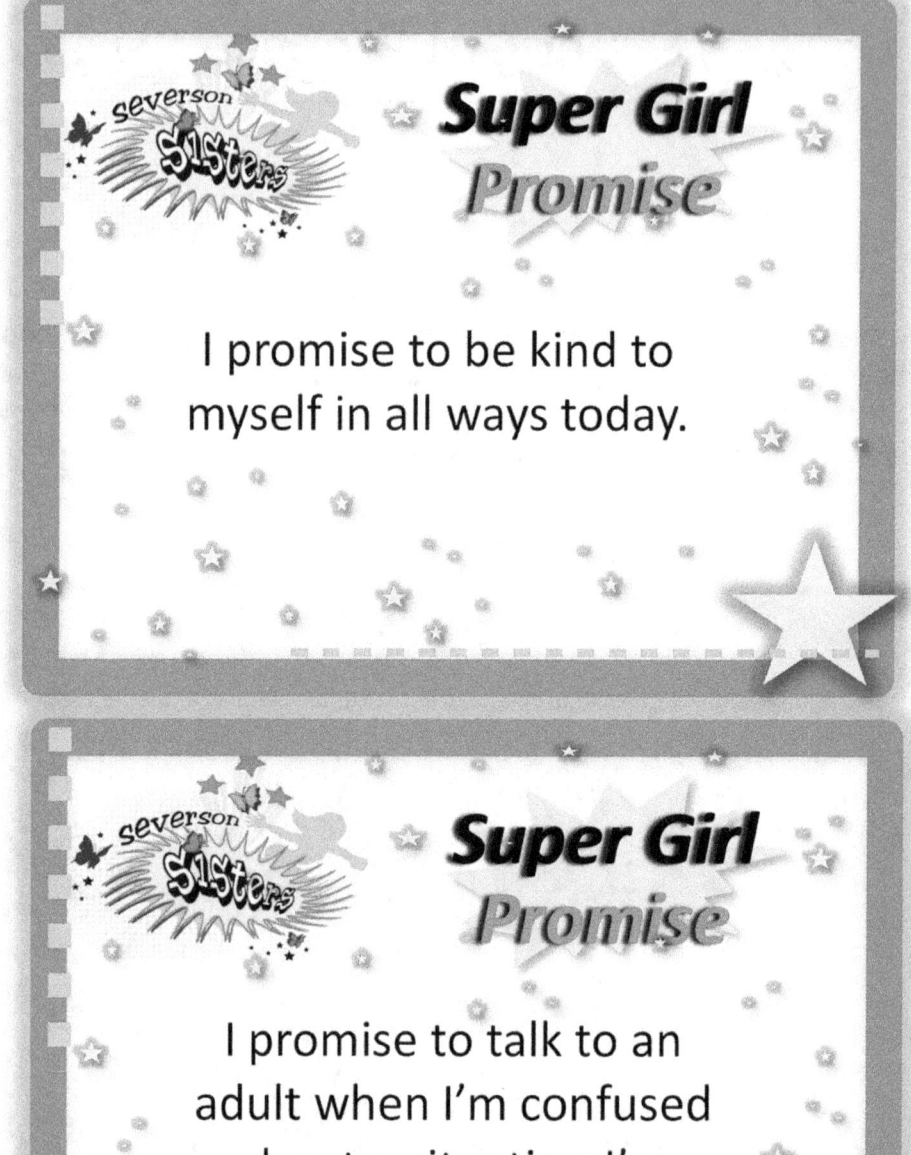

Super Girl
Promise

I promise to be kind to
myself in all ways today.

Super Girl
Promise

I promise to talk to an
adult when I'm confused
about a situation I'm
involved in.

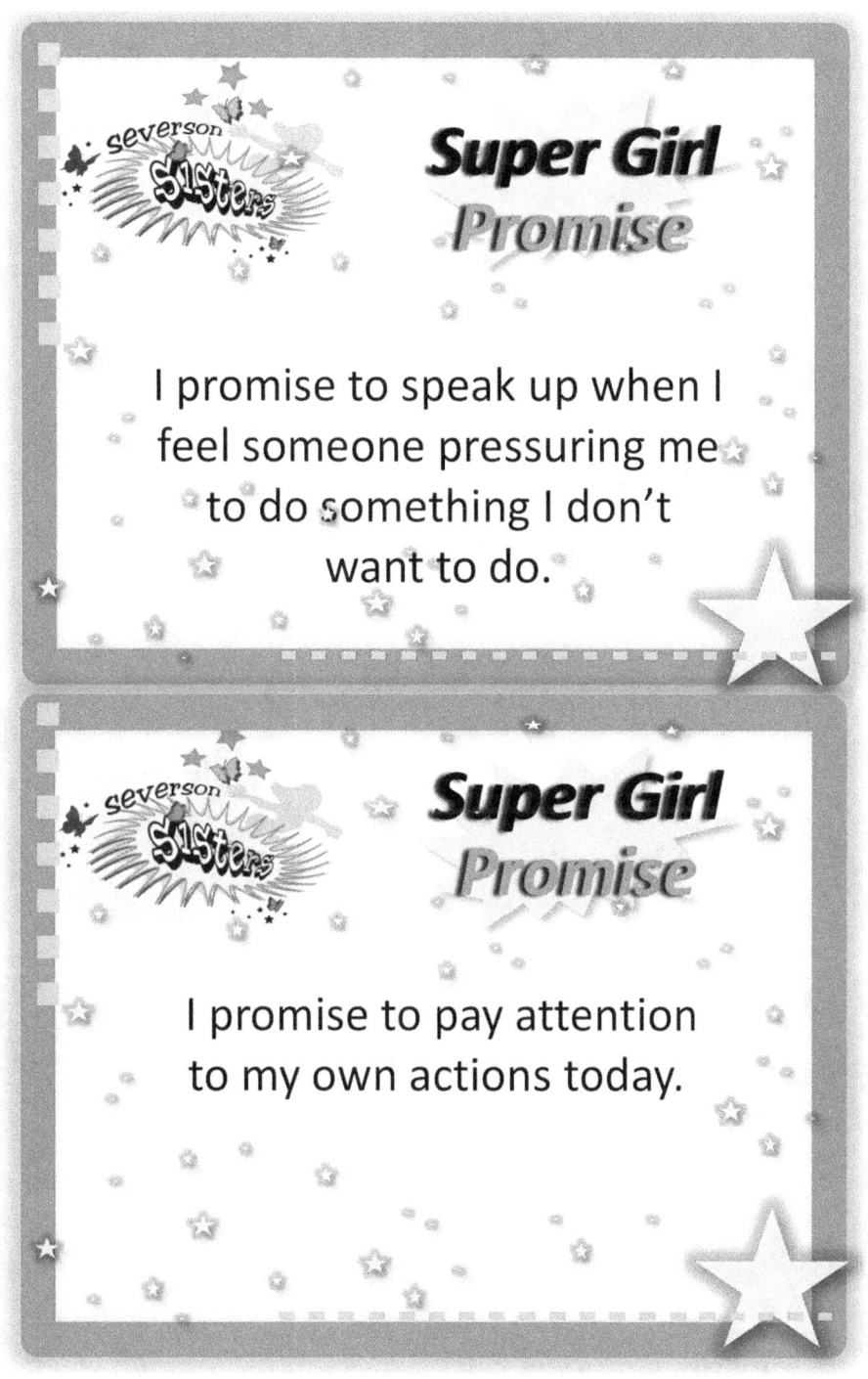

Super Girl
Promise

I promise to speak up when I feel someone pressuring me to do something I don't want to do.

Super Girl
Promise

I promise to pay attention to my own actions today.

Super Girl
Promise

I promise to follow the
rules given to me by
adults when at someone
else's home.

Super Girl
Promise

I promise to think for
myself.

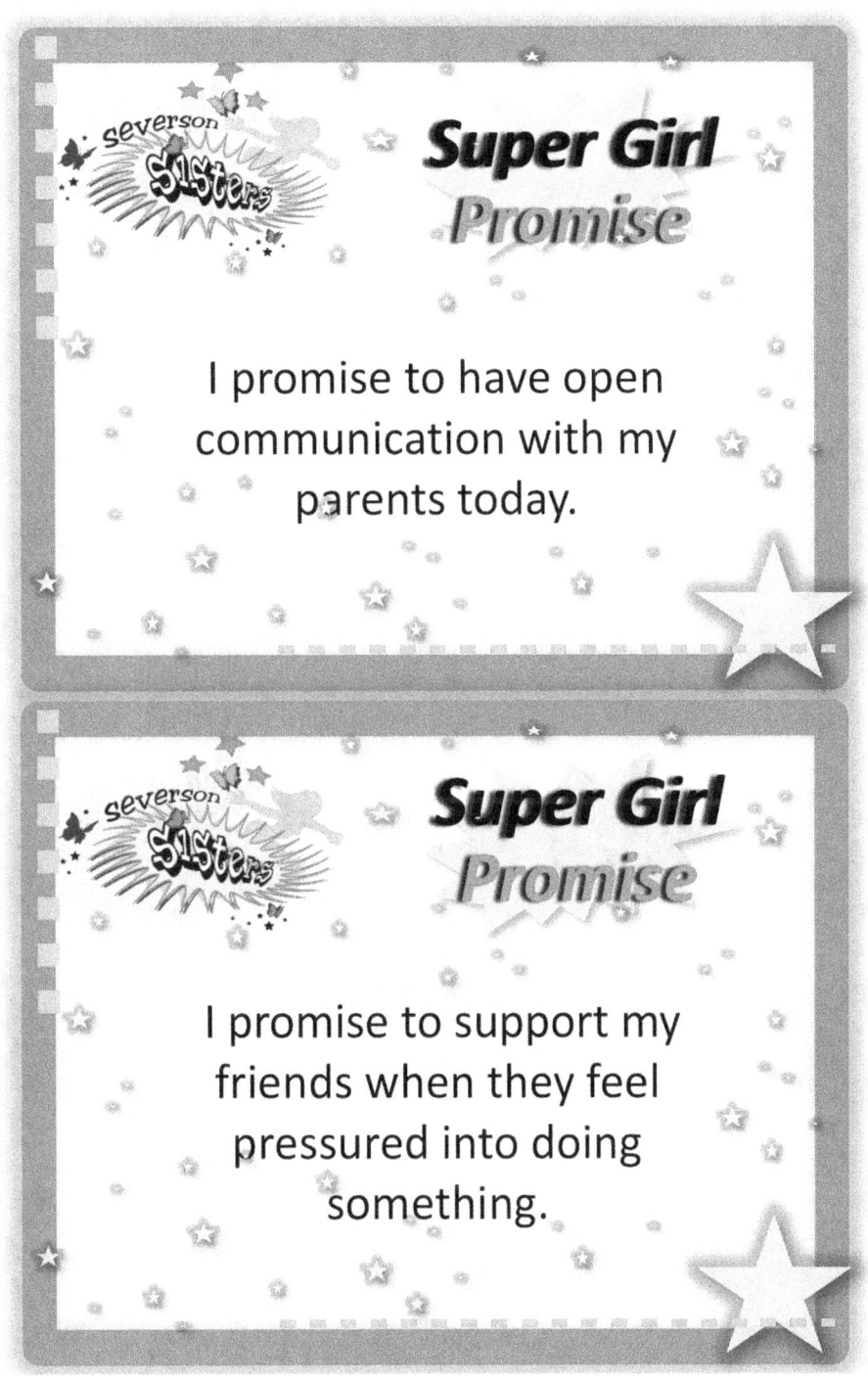

Super Girl Promise

I promise to have open communication with my parents today.

Super Girl Promise

I promise to support my friends when they feel pressured into doing something.

Super Girl
Promise

I promise to stick with my
own set of beliefs.

Super Girl
Promise

I promise to be the kind of
friend I want to have.

Super Girl
Promise

I promise I will walk away when I don't feel comfortable.

Super Girl
Promise

I promise to think before I speak to others.

CHAPTER

4

What's the Deal with Peer Pressure?

What do you think peer pressure is and what does it look like?

What kind of feelings do you have when you experience peer pressure?

Who's affected by peer pressure?

Write down an example of a time you recently experienced peer pressure.

Defining Peer Pressure

Peer pressure is the powerful feeling of pressure from someone of your own age that can push you toward making certain choices, good or bad.

There are two types of peer pressure: unspoken and spoken. Spoken peer pressure is when your friends tell you to do something you otherwise would not do. Write an example of a time you have experienced or seen spoken peer pressure.

Unspoken peer pressure is when you feel pressured to do something even though nobody explicitly told you to do it. Write down an example of a time you witnessed someone do something even though they were not told to do it.

Is all peer pressure bad for you?

Can you give an example of a time when peer pressure helped someone you know?

CHAPTER
5

Girl Talk

Write about a time when you changed your appearance because you felt pressured to do so.

Write about a time you felt bad about yourself because you didn't fit in and thought changing your appearance would help you.

Write about a time you changed your behavior to fit in better.

Write about a time peer pressure had a positive effect in your life.

Write about a time you were pressured by your peers to treat someone a certain way.

CHAPTER 6

Why People Peer Pressure Others

Here are some reasons why people give in to peer pressure:

- To fit in.
- They don't know how to say NO.
- To attract attention.
- Out of fear.
- To get better grades.
- To impress a coach or a teacher.
- To be placed in an advanced class or group.
- To be included in a group (a sports team or club).
- To look a certain way or have a certain body type.
- To learn something (a dance step, a religion, a language).

Write down any other reasons why you think people give in to peer pressure.

Outcomes of Peer Pressure

What would happen if:

- You didn't fit in?

- You said NO.

- You weren't in the spotlight?

- You were fearless?

- You didn't get good grades?

- You let a coach or teacher down?

- You didn't get into an advanced group at school?

- You were left out of a club or team?

- You looked different from your friends?

- You didn't learn a new tool?

What would happen if:
- You gave in to fit in.

- You followed through with what you were asked to do because you were too afraid to say no?

- You attracted attention?

- You acted out of fear?

- You cheated or lied to get better grades?

- You impressed a teacher or a coach?

- You were placed in an advanced class or group?

- You were included in a group (a sports team or club).

- You looked like everyone else?

- You learned something new?

CHAPTER 7

How Do You Deal with Peer Pressure?

Verbal Responses:

- Talk directly to people about what they're asking you to do or say. Make sure they know your feelings.
- Just say no.
- Change the subject of conversation.
- Tell an adult you trust what's going on.
- Tell your friends how you feel and be sure you have backup.

Non-verbal Responses:

- Walk away from the situation.
- Think of the pros and cons of the action and make sure you're able to handle the consequences.
- Reach out to another group of friends to hang out with, and stand by them.
- Go hang out at a safe place until an adult picks you up.

CHAPTER
8

Journaling about Peer Pressure

Keeping track of your emotions and feelings is a good way to review how you felt during certain situations and what you did—or should have done. Here are just some ideas to discuss in your journal to help you make sense of peer pressure.

How would it feel if you did not go along with the crowd? How do you think you would be treated?

Write down what could have happened to you if you had walked away. What would have happened if you had agreed to the peer pressure?

Have you ever put a friend in a position of peer pressure? If so, why did you do it?

CHAPTER
9

Step Up to
Peer Pressure

Stand in a circle with your new Super Girl friends. Have a facilitator read the following statements. When you hear one that you've faced personally, take a step forward.

- Someone tried to use non-verbal peer pressure on me (negative body language).
- Because I did not give in to peer pressure, I lost a friend.
- I was treated badly because I gave in to peer pressure.
- I got into trouble because I gave in to peer pressure.
- I made a new friend because I didn't give in to peer pressure.
- I've stood up for someone else being peer pressured.
- I've told an adult when I faced peer pressure.
- I've felt guilty because I didn't stand up for someone being peer pressured.
- I've felt ashamed for going along with peer pressure.
- I've stopped peer pressure from happening. Period.

CHAPTER
10

Let's Talk about Peer Pressure

Use these conversation starters to talk about peer pressure and how the situations that you discussed in chapter 9 made you feel.

Without using names, share how it feels to hear your peers admit to pressuring others.

How did it feel to see that your Super Girls friends have experienced peer pressure?

What do you think has to happen in order for peer pressure to change?

CHAPTER
11

Peer Pressure Skits

Write and act out the following situation.

A classmate of yours wants to copy your homework. Act out the skit <u>GIVING IN to peer pressure</u>.
Identify the setting, characters, reasons, and emotions within the skit.

Setting:

Characters:

Reasons:

Emotions:

<u>Script:</u>

Write and act out the following situation.

A classmate of yours wants to copy your homework. Act out the skit <u>NOT GIVING IN to peer pressure</u>.
Identify the setting, characters, reasons, and emotions within the skit.

Setting:

Characters:

Reasons:

Emotions:

<u>Script:</u>

Write and act out the following situation.

Your friends want you to ignore and exclude a new student. Act out the skit <u>GIVING IN to peer pressure</u>.
Identify the setting, characters, reasons, and emotions within the skit.

Setting:

Characters:

Reasons:

Emotions:

<u>Script</u>:

Write and act out the following situation.

Your friends want you to ignore and exclude a new student. Act out the skit <u>NOT GIVING IN to peer pressure</u>.
Identify the setting, characters, reasons, and emotions within the skit.

Setting:
Characters:

Reasons:

Emotions:

<u>Script</u>:

Write and act out the following situation.

It's after school and you're going to the mall with your friends. Suddenly they all decide to shop lift at a popular store. Act out the skit GIVING IN to peer pressure.

Identify the setting, characters, reasons, and emotions within the skit.

Setting:

Characters:

Reasons:

Emotions:

Script:

Write and act out the following situation.

It's after school and you're going to the mall with your friends. Suddenly they all decide to shop lift at a popular store. Act out the skit <u>NOT GIVING IN</u> to peer pressure.

Identify the setting, characters, reasons, and emotions within the skit.

Setting:

Characters:

Reasons:

Emotions:

<u>Script</u>:

Write and act out the following situation.

Many of your friends are different from you. Some of them can A.) Wear makeup; B.) Date; C.) Shave. Act out the skit <u>GIVING IN to peer pressure</u>.

Identify the setting, characters, reasons, and emotions within the skit.

Setting:

Characters:

Reasons:

Emotions:

<u>Script:</u>

Write and act out the following situation.

Many of your friends are different from you. Some of them can A.) Wear makeup; B.) Date; C.) Shave. Act out the skit NOT <u>GIVING IN to peer pressure</u>.

Identify the setting, characters, reasons, and emotions within the skit.

Setting:

Characters:

Reasons:

Emotions:

<u>Script:</u>

Confidence Skill Set

Finish these sentences with a word that describes how you're feeling.

1. I feel _____ when I'm left out.
2. I feel _____ when I don't know the answer in school.
3. I feel _____ when I'm invited to a sleepover.
4. I feel _____ when it's time to go to the cafeteria.
5. I feel _____ when I'm going to my gym class.
6. I feel _____ when I'm going to a school dance.
7. I feel _____ on the bus to school.
8. I feel _____ when I get a B on a test.
9. I feel _____ when I volunteer.
10. I feel _____ when I'm in a group project with people I don't know.

Partner up with someone who has the same answer to a question of your choice. Talk about your experiences that led you to that answer. How do you feel talking about it?

Now partner up with someone who has a different answer than you to that same question. Talk to each other about how each of you might be able to handle the situation better in the future. How do you feel after talking about this?

What does a confident person look like?

What qualities does a confident person have?

Is there anything negative about confidence?

Pick three words that describe you.

Think of a time when you didn't feel one of your three words. Did you still feel confident, even though you weren't acting out all three of your best qualities?

On a scale of 0 to 10, how confident do you feel about yourself?

Would you like to be more confident?

What types of things can you do to increase your confidence?

What do you think your strengths are?

As a friend, what qualities do you offer?

"When I'm at home, my strengths are:"

"At school, I'm most confident in:"

Name one area in your life where you feel you most vulnerable.

How can you change your vulnerability into a strength?

Confidence Skill Set

Super Girl, we all make mistakes; that's a part a life! The key to making mistakes is learning from them and how we respond to the situation.

Can you think of a time you said something you didn't mean to say? What happened? How did you respond to the people involved?

How did you feel about yourself after the event?

Next time it happens, what can you do differently?

How do you feel when you have to say, "I'm sorry?"

How do you feel when someone says, "I'm sorry" to you?

Describe the last time you didn't want to say, "I'm sorry." What happened?

Super Girl, remember we all make mistakes. It's important to learn from them and move on. The best lesson is to forgive yourself.

CHAPTER 13

Assertive vs. Aggressive

What does it mean to be assertive? It could look like: Stating what you want in a kind way, making eye contact, knowing what you want, standing your ground.

What does it mean to be aggressive? It could look like: Stating what you want in a bossy way, making commands, being intimidating, yelling, being defensive.

Now let's practice!

Partner up and act out the following situations. Be sure to use your verbal and non-verbal communication tools you learned in Super Girl Guide to Relationships.

1. A classmate has something you really want. Act out this skit asking for the item in an **aggressive** manner.

2. A classmate has something you really want. Act out this skit asking for the item in an **assertive** manner.

3. You want a friend to dress a certain way for school the next day. Act out this situation in an **aggressive** manner.

4. You want a friend to dress a certain way for school the next day. Act out this situation in an **assertive** manner.

Assertive vs. Aggressive

What was it like to have someone speak to you aggressively?

What differences did you notice between aggressive and assertive?

How did both make you feel?

How do assertive people make you feel?

How do you respond to assertive people?

How do aggressive people make you feel?

How do you respond to aggressive people?

How do you let aggressive or assertive people know if they make you feel a certain way?

Super Girl, here is how to deal with aggressive and assertive people.

- Just because they increase the volume or tone of their voice doesn't mean you need to.
- When someone gets in your personal space, take a step back.
- Wait until the other person is done talking and then ask them what's wrong so you can better understand the problem.
- Stay calm by counting to 10 in your mind and taking a breath.
- Think about how you want to respond and then speak.
- Speak respectfully to the other person in the same way you would want to be spoken to.

CHAPTER

14

What's the Deal with the Clique?

How would you define a clique?

Do you think cliques are good? Why or why not?

What type of cliques do you see at your school?

If you're in a clique right now, what does your clique do together?

How does one get into your clique?

Do you allow everyone into your clique?

Super Girl: Cliques are a group of people who like the same things but don't allow others to easily join. Cliques are not the Super Girl way. Write out how you'd respond to the following scenario.

You're interested in being friends with a group of girls who all dress differently than you do. How do you approach them? What do you say if they don't accept you? How do you feel?

You're in a clique with a group of girls who all dress the same way. A girl who dresses differently than you all approaches you and wants to be your friend. How do you feel when she wants to join when you know she doesn't fit in?

You want to be friends with a girl your clique doesn't accept. Your clique starts to peer pressure you to not accept her. What do you say?

Speak Up, Super Girl!

Think about who you are and what you stand for. You're an awesome, authentic Super Girl and don't need to be friends with girls who can't see that.

- Write down three short, confident statements that you will say to the girls in the clique who don't accept you. Examples are: **"How would you feel if I said that to you?"** or **"I'm glad I know who you really are. I don't need this."**

  _____ .

  _____ .

  _____ .

- Say the three sentences you wrote above. Then confidently walk away.
- Tell a teacher or other adult you trust at school about what happened.
- Next, be sure to tell your parent or guardian what happened. Tell them who was involved and what was said.
- Take out your journal. Answer these questions:
  1. How did you feel when you were not accepted?
  2. How did you feel when you responded to the clique?
  3. What are your thoughts about the situation?
  4. Is there anything you would do differently?

Super Girl, it's so important to be nice to yourself! Write down three things you can do for yourself to feel better right now. Do all three of them.

Real Friends vs. Cliques

Do you think the girls in your clique are real friends of yours?

Write down key characteristics of a real friend.

How do your real friends make you feel?

Do you feel this way about the girls in your clique?

Do the girls in your clique have your key characteristics for being a real friend?

Draw a stick figure to represent each person in your circle of friends. Write a word under each stick figure to describe each friend in your circle.

What's the Deal with the Clique?

So what does your circle of friends look like? Does it look healthy?

Are the people you call friends your real friends?

What do you think are the best qualities for your Super Girl Code of Membership?

Authentic	Respectful	Kind	Caring	Loyal
Awesome	Super	Truthful	Mean	Bossy
Selfish	Unfair			

In a clique and not sure how to deal with it? Be sure to talk to your Super Girl Facilitator today.

CHAPTER
15

Let's Talk about Judgment

Explain why you judged someone in a clique?

How have you been judged?

How did you change your behavior or your attitude because you were judged?

How did you feel about your change?

What was the result? Did it lead it to something positive or negative?

Alright, Super Girl, get ready to Style Your Super Girl.

Pair off with the Super Girl to your left and write down four words that define how you see her Super Girl "Selfie."

Now write down four words to define the Super Girl in real life.

What similarities do you see between the Super Girl "Selfie" and the Super Girl?

What differences do you see between the two?

Share with your partner how you felt judging her Selfie.

Straight Talk, Super Girl

Describe a time you wore something to get compliments.

What did you wear, what was said, and how did you feel?

Where did the inspiration for your outfit come from?

Have you chosen an outfit and received negative feedback? What was said and did you feel judged?

Have you ever posted or sent a photo of yourself to get a response from someone?

What were the judgments made about your photo—both positive and negative?

Describe a time you felt peer pressured to dress a certain way for a photo because of someone famous.

How do you feel when a friend of yours is receiving negative comments about how she looks?

Grab a Magazine, Super Girl

Look at some magazines and choose images of female celebrities or models dressed provocatively and/or engaging in provocative acts.

What words would you use to define the images and the acts you see?

CHAPTER
16

Joy, Hope, and Grace

Dear Super Girl,

My family and I were at a Fourth of July barbeque over the summer. Everyone I knew was there. My friends and I were all swimming, and our parents were all standing around talking. One of my friends dared me to go get a drink out of the adult refrigerator instead of the kid refrigerator.

Joy

Super Girl, what would you do next?

What are the consequences of getting an adult beverage?

What are the consequences of saying no to your friends?

What are the pros and cons of going along with dares?

What are the pros and cons of saying no to dares?

Dear Super Girl,

I was with a friend at a mall. We were looking at creative art supplies that we wanted to use to decorate T-shirts for a dress-up day at school. We each had $8 to spend, but supplies we wanted to buy were $10. My friend grabbed the supplies she needed, hid them, and walked out of the store.

Hope

What happens next, Super Girl?

What would you say to your friend who steals?

How could you get into trouble when you're with someone who breaks a law?

Would you tell on your friend who steals?

What are the pros and cons of going along with stealing?

What are the pros and cons of saying no to stealing?

Dear Super Girl,

I was at a sleepover with about 10 girls when I was in seventh grade. As soon as my friend's parents went to bed, she suggested we sneak out of the house. I felt really uncomfortable disobeying, but most of the girls wanted to go. We went to a party down the street at another classmate's house. We stayed at the party for a little while. One friend and I wanted to go home, and the rest of the girls wanted to stay at the party. When we got back into the house, my friend's parents were waiting up for us. We were in so much trouble. Her parents made us tell them where the rest of the girls were. All of us had to go home that night.

Grace

What do you think happened to the girls next?

Write down dangerous scenarios that could have happened.

What are the pros and cons of sneaking out?

What are the pros and cons of staying in?

Act Out an Alternative

Write and act out alternative situations to all three sceneries described by Joy, Hope, and Grace.

Joy

Setting:

Characters:

Reasons:

Emotions:

Script:

Hope

Setting:

Characters:

Reasons:

Emotions:

Script:

Grace

Setting:

Characters:

Reasons:

Emotions:

Script:

CHAPTER 17

Setting Boundaries

A boundary is defined by rules that we have for ourselves about what is acceptable behavior and what we expect from others.

You should set boundaries when you're uncomfortable with certain people.

You should set boundaries when you don't agree with someone else's actions.

You should set boundaries when you feel pressured.

Who are the closest people to you?

Movement of Supporters

This exercise is great for you to see how important personal boundaries are. Follow the next steps and be sure to have fun!

1. Write down your name on a piece of paper and place it in the center of the room.

2. Next write down on nametags the names of 5–8 Super Girl Supporters you have in your life.

3. Next place each of the nametags on the floor. Stagger them so that the person you trust the most is closest to your name. Be sure their nametags are clearly seen.

4. When you're done, you should have created an appropriate boundaries circle accordingly to how close they are to you.

5. Tell the Super Girl Supporters why you placed them in their positions.

Personal Space

Now that you know what your boundaries are, let's put them into action.

What would you do if someone from your outer circle was trying to get into your inner circle?

How do you create space with someone who continues to make decisions, betrays your trust, or peer pressures you into things you don't want to do?

What are you going to do about people who don't respect your boundaries?

Write down two sentences you can say to someone when you're setting a boundary.

Let's Prepare

Sometimes, setting boundaries is difficult. Staying true to yourself is so important. Often times, though, you may upset someone by doing it.

Here are key things to remember:

1. Setting boundaries may upset people in your life. When you upset people, it's important to come back to your Power Words and remind yourself why you're a Super Girl.

2. List out friends you have that you can go talk to. Losing a friend or two is hard, but look at it as an opportunity to make two new friends.

3. Talk to a teacher, parent, or guardian to help you. That person may be able to help you find new ways to make new friends.

If ... Then ... Because

In the boxes below, you will learn how to set a boundary. Once you identify that someone is making you feel uncomfortable, you will identify how you will choose to respond to them. Don't forget to tell them why it is important to you and how it makes you feel.

If... (identify the behavior that makes you feel uncomfortable)	Then... (identify your reaction)	Because it makes me feel... (identify how the behavior makes you feel)
If my friends peer pressure you into disrespecting a classmate.	Then I will tell them "no" and go tell the teacher.	Because it makes me feel _____.
If my friend tells me that I need to wear something that I am uncomfortable wearing.	Then I will _____ _____	Because it makes me feel _____.
If _____	Then I will _____ _____	Because it makes me feel guilty.
If _____	Then I won't be your friend anymore.	Because it makes me feel proud.
If _____	Then I will _____ _____	Because it makes me feel _____.
If _____	Then I will _____ _____	Because it makes me feel_____

Ready for New Friends, Super Girl?

We know that sometimes it can be hard to make new friends.

We came up with questions for you to ask when you are talking to new people for the first time.

Go around your Super Girl group and ask as many people as you can ALL of these questions!

Write down the name of each Super Girl you talk to AND her answers. Be sure you notice which girls share your common interests.

- Who's your favorite singer?

- What's your favorite TV show?

- Are you in any sports?

- Do you play an instrument?

- Do you have any pets?

- If you could have a superpower, what would it be?

- What do you want to be when you grow up?

- What's your favorite subject in school?

- Who's your favorite teacher?

- What's your favorite family tradition?

- Where would you go on vacation?

- What's your favorite food?

- Do you have any siblings?

- Do you ever volunteer?

- What's your favorite part of the school year so far?

Let's Practice Setting Boundaries

Pick three of the below practices that you feel most comfortable with to learn how to set boundaries.

- When someone gets in your personal space and you feel uncomfortable, take a step back.
- Decline invitations politely when you are uncomfortable being around certain people.
- Always make sure an adult is around you if you're uncomfortable.
- Wait until the other person is done talking and then respond. If they interrupt you, say, "I let you finish talking; please let me finish talking."
- If you feel someone in your life continues to cross your boundaries, you may have to end the friendship. Ask your Super Girl Facilitator for the right sentence to say if this happens.
- Speak respectfully to the other person in the same way you would want to be spoken to.
- Just because other people increase the volume or tone of their voice doesn't mean you need to.
- Be sure you're aware of other people's boundaries and be respectful.
- Pick the right time to set a boundary.

Moving Boundaries

Stand on the opposite side of the room and make confident statements to people walking toward you as they get too close.

CHAPTER 18

Peer Pressured into Attention

Super Girl, would you like to be noticed? Let's talk about it!

What type of attention are you looking for? Circle all that you want to have.

- Friendship
- Compliments
- Hand holding in the halls
- A date to the dance
- A kiss
- Acceptance
- A gift

Write out all of the seven statements that you identity with in the appropriate column below.

I wanted to.	I saw someone doing it.	All my friends were doing it.

Write down what happened when you experienced the following scenarios.

- You gained a new friendship.

- You received compliments.

- You held hands with someone in the hallway.

- You went to the dance with someone.

- You kissed someone you wanted to.

- You were accepted for who you are.

- You received a gift.

How would your self-worth change if more people noticed you?

How did gaining a new friend make you feel?

How did receiving compliments make you feel?

How did you feel holding hands in the hallway?

How did you feel going to the dance with someone?

How did kissing someone make you feel?

What did you feel when you were accepted?

How did it feel when you received a gift?

Peer Pressure Skill Set

Create three positive statements that you can repeat to yourself every morning and night.

I'm pretty because_____.

I'm unique because _____.

I'm lovable because _____.

I'm smart because _____.

I'm an individual because _____.

New Super Girl Selfie

Pick your favorite Positive Statement from your Appearance Peer Pressure Skill Set.

Grab some creative supplies and decorate a sign that highlights your statement.

Now take a new Selfie!

CHAPTER 19

Stars and Wishes & Personal Promises

How we talk to one another is very important.

We send you stars for your work today and wishes for what you're going to do tomorrow!

- **Stars** are compliments you give to your Super Girl sisters for what they did today. It's a personal compliment you give to someone else and it is NOT based on her appearance or popularity.
- **Wishes** are comments that support your Super Girl sisters for something they will do tomorrow or later in the week. These, too, are very personal, both from you and to her.

Here are some awesome examples of **Stars**!

- I Star you for your honesty today.
- I Star you for your performance in music class today.
- I Star you for your bravery.

Here are some awesome examples of **Wishes**!

- I Wish you good luck on the math test tomorrow.
- I Wish for you to make up with your friend tomorrow.
- I Wish you a safe trip to your grandma's house this weekend.

Now it's your turn!
Send a Star to the Super Girl on your right!
Send a Wish to the Super Girl on your left!

Personal Promises

The last part of our workbook involves the Personal Promise. Cut out all of the Personal Promises we provided to you. These are here for you to make your own positive affirmations.

Create a Personal Promise around your home life, school life, family, and friends.

Have fun and get creative! Write down a Personal Promise every day for one month and be sure to DO that Personal Promise!

Great job, Super Girl!

Severson Sisters Tips to Improve Self-Esteem

Positive affirmations

Girls have a tendency to compare themselves to other girls, whether they are peers or celebrities. This is a slippery slope that can lead to unhealthy habits. Every time you compare yourself to another girl, write down and read aloud something positive you love about yourself and something positive you love about your life. Make sure it's something different every time. Get used to expanding your list of loves! Find a cute notebook that you can use for these exercises. Have fun with it and make this a habit.

Powerful and open communication

Talk, talk, talk. One great way to open dialogue with your parent or a close friend is by creating a dream board. Flip through magazines and tear out images or words you're drawn to. It's a great conversation starter that will lead to what you're feeling about your life. Dream boards provide great inspiration for who we will become. Make this a monthly task and have fun with it. Let the conversation flow!

Afterschool activity

Afterschool activities provide a structure to life that keeps children engaged. Research shows that youth involved in academics, the arts, sports, or community activities are more likely to develop confidence and good self-esteem. Find a program that fits your interest and enroll. And as your interests change, your afterschool activity should, too. Always be engaged in something you're passionate about every school year.

Healthy habits

It's important to love our bodies regardless of the shape, weight, or differences between us and our peers. Loving our bodies comes down to forming positive and healthy habits for the mind, body, and soul. Ask for help to learn how to form a healthy relationship with food. Ask your parent to make meals from ingredients bought at a local farmers market and pitch in to help. By helping form a healthy relationship with food, you can avoid pitfalls with body-image issues as you continue to evolve. By fueling your body better, you'll feel better, which sparks great self-esteem.

Dedicate time to interests

Girls are busy! But whether it's a weekly or bi-weekly routine, dedicate time to personal interests that you can work on at home. By creating something for yourself, by yourself, you have the opportunity to shine and display your individuality without worrying about peer influence that might stifle your sparkly self. Who knows, maybe this can be a fun project the entire household can get into! Pretty soon you'll have the next *So You Think You Can Dance* team on your hands!

Resources

Stop Bullying
http://www.stopbullying.gov/

Pacer's National Bullying Prevention Center
http://www.pacer.org/bullying/?gclid=CLTSgOLkrKsCFQJUgwodKjr_2g

Teens Against Bullying
http://www.pacerteensagainstbullying.org/#/home

Stomp Out Bullying
http://www.stompoutbullying.org

Empowered Kidz
http://www.empoweredkidz.com/

Severson Sisters
http://www.seversonsisters.org/

About the Authors

In January of 2011, at the age of 32, with only her savings and 401K dollars in hand, Carrie Severson took a leap of faith and launched Severson Sisters, an empowerment organization for females headquartered in Phoenix. The organizations mission is to inspire girls to live their life as their authentic, awesome, super self. Severson Sisters plays a role in the lives of Super Girls to help them become confident Super Women who will lead their communities.

Holly (Severson) Hammerquist has a Bachelor's Degree in Elementary Education and a Master's Degree in curriculum. She brings her education and experience to the Super Girl curriculum and workbooks. Holly makes sure that the girls enrolled in the Severson Sisters Super Girl Program always show their true colors.

Shirley Barna has a passion for psychology and working with children. She has over 10 years of experience working with children, families, and adults in the capacity of a counselor, problem solver, and advocate. Shirley received a Bachelor of Science degree in Psychology with a minor in Family Studies at Northern Arizona University.

Anne McGill is a licensed psychologist who has worked with children, adults, and families in a variety of different roles including counseling, psychological testing and research. She has functioned as an advocate for children, adults, and the elderly, always focusing on positively affecting their sense of well-being. Her experience includes providing services for a myriad of settings, including disabled students at state universities, intake and crisis management at local hospitals, psychological and counseling services for local schools and social service agencies, and conducting clinical drug trials for mood disorders.

Brittany Lang has researched various mental health topics at Southern Methodist University and Arizona State University and continues to be passionate about research and clinical intervention. Brittany has worked with children, adults, and families in various clinical and research settings, and she is currently managing a facility that provides therapeutic services to women with psychiatric and substance abuse diagnoses. Through her own personal experiences and also through her work, Brittany became passionate about empowering young girls to be their "Super Girl" selves!

Journal

Journal

Journal

Journal

Journal

Journal

Journal

Journal

Journal

Journal

Journal

Journal

Journal

Journal

Journal

Journal

Journal

www.ingramcontent.com/pod-product-compliance
Lightning Source LLC
Chambersburg PA
CBHW081148280526
45787CB00008B/3257